D0816640

The Italian Americans

RICHARD BOWEN

WE CAME TO AMERICA

MASON CREST PUBLISHERS • PHILADELPHIA

The leaning tower of Pisa is one of the most popular tourist attractions in Italy. An extensive renovation project, intended to keep the tower from toppling over, was completed in 2002.

The Italian Americans

RICHARD BOWEN

WE CAME TO AMERICA

MASON CREST PUBLISHERS • PHILADELPHIA

Mason Crest Publishers
370 Reed Road
Broomall PA 19008
www.masoncrest.com

Copyright © 2003 by Mason Crest Publishers. All rights reserved.

First printing

1 3 5 7 9 8 6 4 2

Library of Congress Cataloging-in-Publication Data
on file at the Library of Congress

ISBN 1-59084-114-X

Table of Contents

WE CAME TO AMERICA

America's Ethnic Heritage

Barry Moreno, librarian

Statue of Liberty/

Ellis Island National Monument

Ethnic diversity is one of the most striking characteristics of the American identity. In the United States the Bureau of the Census officially recognizes 122 different ethnic groups. North America's population had grown by leaps and bounds, starting with the American Indian tribes and nations—the continent's original people—and increasing with the arrival of the European colonial migrants who came to these shores during the 16th and 17th centuries. Since then, millions of immigrants have come to America from every corner of the world.

But the passage of generations and the great distance of America from the "Old World"—Europe, Africa, and Asia—has in some cases separated immigrant peoples from their roots. The struggle to succeed in America made it easy to forget past traditions. Further, the American spirit of freedom, individualism, and equality gave Americans a perspective quite different from the view of life shared by residents of the Old World.

Immigrants of the 19th and 20th centuries recognized this at once. Many tried to "Americanize" themselves by tossing away their peasant clothes and dressing American-style even before reaching their new homes in the cities or the countryside of America. It was not so easy to become part of America's culture, however. For many immigrants, learning English was quite a hurdle. In fact, most older immigrants clung to the old ways, preferring to speak their native languages and follow their familiar customs and traditions. This was easy to do when ethnic neighborhoods abounded in large North American cities like New York, Montreal, Philadelphia, Chicago, Toronto, Boston, Cleveland, St. Louis, New Orleans and San Francisco. In rural areas, farm families—many of them Scandinavian, German, or Czech—established their own tightly knit communities. Thus foreign languages and dialects, religious beliefs, Old World customs, and certain class distinctions flourished.

The most striking changes occurred among the children of immigrants, whose hopes and dreams were different from those of their parents. They began breaking away from the Old World customs, perhaps as a reaction to the embarrassment of being labeled "foreigner." They badly wanted to be Americans, and assimilated more easily than their parents and grandparents. They learned to speak English without a foreign accent, to dress and act like other Americans. The assimilation of the children of immigrants was encouraged by social contact—games, schools, jobs, and military service—which further broke down the barriers between immigrant groups and hastened the process of Americanization. Along the way, many family traditions were lost or abandoned.

Today, the pride that Americans have in their ethnic roots is one of the abiding strengths of both the United States and Canada. It shows that the theory which called America a "melting pot" of the world's people was never really true. The thought that a single "American" would emerge from the combination of these peoples has never happened, for Americans have grown more reluctant than ever before to forget the struggles of their ethnic forefathers. The growth of cultural studies and genealogical research indicates that Americans are anxious not to entirely lose this identity, whether it is English, French, Chinese, African, Mexican, or some other group. There is an interest in tracing back the family line as far as records or memory will take them. In a sense, this has made Americans a divided people; proud to be Americans, but proud also of their ethnic roots.

As a result, many Americans have welcomed a new identity, that of the hyphenated American. This unique description has grown in usage over the years and continues to grow as more Americans recognize the importance of family heritage. In the end, this is an appreciation of America's great cultural heritage and its richness of its variety.

A man harvests grapes for Chianti wine in vineyards that were once owned by the Italian political philosopher Machiavelli. Italy has a long history of wine production.

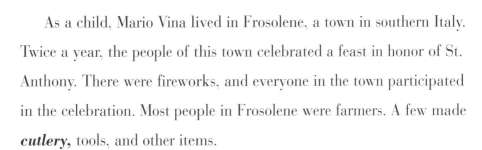

1 The Story of Mario Vina

As a child, Mario Vina lived in Frosolene, a town in southern Italy. Twice a year, the people of this town celebrated a feast in honor of St. Anthony. There were fireworks, and everyone in the town participated in the celebration. Most people in Frosolene were farmers. A few made **cutlery,** tools, and other items.

Mario's family lived in an apartment above a wine shop. The family cooked most of their food and heated their living quarters using an open fireplace. "My mother used to make…lovely bread," Mario recalls. "We used to go to the mill and grind the grains. Then she'd take it to a place in town where they used to cook it in the ovens." The apartment in which they lived had no plumbing, so they had to carry water in buckets from the town's fountain back to their home.

Mario's grandfather made cheese. Mario's father was a woodcutter who decided to go to America in search of a better life. This was in the early 20th century. Mario's father could not afford to take his family, so they were left behind in Frosolene. Mario's mother cared for an elderly neighbor woman to make money while he was gone. Mario went to school in a one-room schoolhouse where he took first, second, and third grades.

In America, Mario's father got a job in a cast-iron shop in Middletown, Connecticut. He sent money to the family for their voyage. But when Mario's grandfather fell from a horse and became ill, his mother spent all of the money for doctors and medicine. Eventually, the grandfather died. Then Mario's father sent them tickets for the boat. Mario said, "I was glad I was going to America, but then I was sorry I left all my friends." His mother packed the family's belongings in a trunk and sent it off to America.

The family traveled by stagecoach, horse and carriage, and then by train to the port city of Naples, Italy. Mario had never seen a train, a boat, or the ocean before this. When they arrived in Naples, they boarded the boat and stayed overnight on it. They sailed the next day. Their tickets were for the *steerage* class, which meant they all stayed together in the lowest part of the ship.

When they got on board, Mario was separated from his mother and the rest of the family. He was 11 years old and did not like this, so he began to search for them. When he finally found them, his mother said, "I don't have enough room for you to sleep here." A lady nearby said she had enough room, so Mario stayed with her.

Mario's mother was seasick the entire voyage; almost everyone was. And the boat was crowded. Mario loved it, however, and was sad when the journey ended. When they arrived, he said to himself, "Well, this is it. This is America."

The boat arrived on the Fourth of July, so they saw fireworks as they entered New York harbor. Doctors on the boat checked their ears, eyes, and hearts. Fortunately, all the members of Mario's family passed the examination. Then they took a ferryboat to Ellis Island.

An Italian peasant family travels in their horse-drawn cart. This method of transportation is still used in parts of Italy, where Old World traditions resist the changes that industrialization and modernization bring.

Ellis Island, the point of entry for millions of immigrants from 1892 to 1954, is located in New York Harbor. The building compound has since been renovated and is now an immigration museum.

Mario remembers the people on Ellis Island gave everyone a nametag. They also served them sandwiches. He had never eaten a sandwich before. They got on another ferryboat and went to Battery Park. That was the first time Mario was close to the Statue of Liberty. He recalls, "I had seen pictures of it in different books in Italy. I thought it was a beautiful monument, one of the most beautiful things I've ever seen."

When they got to Battery Park, they saw two men walking down the stairs toward them. It was their father and a friend. When his mother saw them, she cried out, "It's Papa!" They hugged and kissed; his father hugged Mario and the other children and patted Mario on the back. Mario had forgotten what his father looked like.

The family took a train to Middletown, Connecticut. When they got there, Mario's father gave him something he had never seen before. It was a baseball glove and bat. Mario asked his father, "What are these for?" His father replied, "You play with these. It's a game. It's called baseball." ✸

A couple hoes a field on their farm. Agriculture remains an important way of life in Italy, especially in the south, where the climate in the lowlands is just right for cultivating crops.

Why They Came

A number of factors forced Italians to leave their country and *emigrate* to North America. It is helpful to look back at the history of the region known as Italy to understand these factors.

The northern and southern parts of Italy are different in many ways. Northern Italy, because of its climate and European influence, is more industrialized. Southern Italy is warmer, its climate more suitable for farming.

During the late 1700s, an *aristocracy* made up of kings, queens, princes, and land barons ruled most of Europe. The revolutionary ideas that brought about a *republican* form of government in the United States were also forcing changes in France, where a revolution occurred. This resulted in a French republican government, which in turn encouraged changes in other European countries. In countries like Italy, ideas of freedom and prosperity for all were aroused. France's government was defeated in the early 1800s, however, and the king was brought back to the throne. This led to the *repression* of the reforms that had taken place in France as well as in neighboring countries.

During this time, the northwestern corner of present-day Italy was the only independent Italian state. It was called the Piedmont, with its capital city Turin. Austria, whose rulers were from a family called the Hapsburgs, controlled the rest of Italy. The Hapsburgs divided Italy into eight separate states. They made trade between these states difficult by charging high *tariffs*. In addition, they instituted tariffs inside each state. The tariffs made internal and external trade difficult, which was one of the main reasons why most people remained poor.

Only a few of the people who worked the land actually owned it. Most of the land was owned by ***absentee landlords***, primarily the nobility and the Catholic church. The tenant farmers paid high rent and received low wages. Peasants who did own land either lived too far away from it to have a normal family life, or the plot was too small to provide enough income. During the 1800s, when most of Europe was adopting modern methods of farming and manufacturing, the nobility refused to do so in Italy. Thus, Italy continued to be a beautiful, but poor, land.

Over 90 percent of the population of southern Italy at this time was farmers. Although the climate is warm, the land is not particularly well suited for farming. The terrain is mostly mountains—too high to be good farmland. Another problem was water: most of the south, called the *Mezzogiorno*, does not have enough rainfall. When precipitation does occur, it comes in the winter, not during the growing season. In addition, the *Mezzogiorno* does not have many deep, navigable rivers, which makes transporting goods to market difficult and expensive.

In southern Italy in the late 1800s, a dramatic change was taking place in the environment. While many acres in the south remained fertile and green, in some areas people began to cut the forests at an unprecedented rate. This resulted in the soil gradually washing away, causing mudslides and avalanches and eventually leaving exposed rock where crops could not grow.

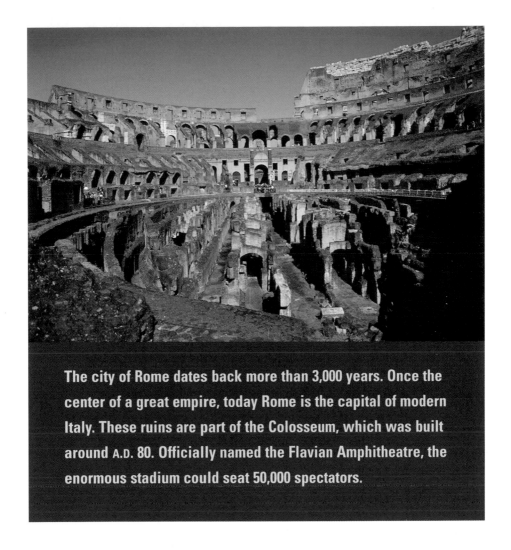

The city of Rome dates back more than 3,000 years. Once the center of a great empire, today Rome is the capital of modern Italy. These ruins are part of the Colosseum, which was built around A.D. 80. Officially named the Flavian Amphitheatre, the enormous stadium could seat 50,000 spectators.

Also in the late 1800s, an epidemic of malaria swept through the southern region. Malaria is a disease carried by mosquitoes, which breed in low-lying areas. Because most good farmland was located on the lower plains, this meant the peasants who wanted to avoid contracting the disease could not live near the land they farmed. Instead, they had to spend time traveling between the villages located on higher ground and the fields. This made farming much less *profitable*.

Camillo Benso, count di Cavour was the organizer, politician, and diplomat who made the union of Italy a reality. Before his time the Italian peninsula was made up of scattered independent states, but it was the count di Cavour who created the modern united Italy.

Homes in the south were often no more than shacks without windows or a chimney. The people had to share the house with chickens, and, if they had money enough to buy one, a pig. Plumbing was a novelty in the cities and almost nonexistent in the countryside. Food was in short supply and very simple. Tools were old and out-of-date. Farming methods were not scientific, and crop yields were not great.

In early times, emigration out of the country was not permitted, so even if a poor person had the money to leave, he or she often could not. The rigid social customs of the time did not allow people born in poverty to advance into a higher class. Poor people seemed *resigned* to their way of life because there were few alternatives. The rulers controlled nearly everything, including the government, the land, and the money supply. They made the laws (only two percent of the population voted), and often forced taxes on those least able to pay—the masses of poor people. For example, the poor had to pay 40 times the actual value of salt because of the many taxes imposed on this **commodity**.

In 1866, the Italian states joined Prussia to defeat Austria. This gave Italy control of Venice, one of its most important cities. On July 2, 1871, five years later, after a series of military and political maneuvers, Italian troops entered Rome, and Italy was declared an independent, united nation.

This did not necessarily mean an improvement in conditions, however. In fact, conditions for the poor actually became worse after independence. The population continued to grow, but production of food and other necessities remained about the same. This was because the middle and upper classes still maintained control and continued to

A young boy stands barefoot in an Italian street. The gap between the rich and poor in Europe was a problem for years, and the opportunity to start a new life in America was irresistible to many poverty-stricken Italians.

Gondolas rock gently in a waterway in Venice, Italy. Once a powerful city-state that controlled commerce between Europe and Asia during the Middle Ages, Venice today is a popular tourist attraction. The city was built on a series of small islands in a lagoon of the Adriatic Sea. Venice is known for the canals that flow past the city's buildings.

resist change. Some called it a "missed revolution," meaning that when Italy became independent, a genuine social and economic change could have occurred but did not.

While a middle class began to develop around this time in countries like France and England, Italy was still a *stratified* country. Rich land-owners comprised about two percent of the population. Ten percent of the population consisted of *bureaucrats* and professional people, who served the upper class. The remaining population, 88 percent, were peasants.

Those who formed the government of independent Italy were almost all northern Italians. The father of modern Italy, Count Camillo Cavour, had never traveled farther south than Florence and intended to create a country only comprised of the northern section. The southern area was almost unknown to him and the other rulers. When they found out about the poverty in the south, they concluded that all that was necessary to solve this problem was good government. Good government to the poor of the south meant more freedom, more food and less poverty. To the rulers, however, it meant imposing more taxes. It also meant mandatory enlistment in the army for young men. In addition, the laws that the new government enacted allowed commodities and manufactured items into the country from abroad, which substantially lowered prices, ruining farming and manufacturing in the *Mezzogiorno*. Tropical fruit production in Florida and California increased rapidly at this time, which reduced the demand for fruit from southern Italy. American and Russian grains flooded into the country, which drastically reduced the price of domestic grains. The government also opposed the Catholic church, which was one

In the southern part of Italy between 1860 and 1870, out of 14 million people, around five million—over one-third of the south's total population—left the country to seek a better life in other parts of the world. Between 1881 and 1911, over 11 million people, about one-quarter of the entire population, left Italy.

of the few institutions actively helping the poor during this time.

Some industry was developing in northern Italy, especially around the cities of Genoa, Turin, and Milan. Factories in these cities provided jobs for the peasants in the north but could not sustain the southern peasants as well.

Many poor Italians simply could not wait for economic and social conditions to improve, so they decided to seek better opportunities elsewhere. They saw leaving the country as a real alternative to continued poverty and hopelessness.

From 1861 to 1881, the government generally did not allow people to emigrate. Therefore, only about 12,000 people left the country during this time. Many of these were northern Italians who left for other areas of Europe, worked for a while, and returned home. In 1880, there were fewer than 100,000 Italians in the United States, out of a total population of 50 million Americans.

From 1881 to 1901, the government did not oppose emigration, but it did not encourage it either. The result was that only about six percent of the immigrants to North America were from Italy. Following 1901, the government began to take an active role in helping people emigrate and seek a better life. With the population growing faster than the economy, which meant the poor people were less able to provide for themselves and were becoming more of a burden, the government saw emigration as a "safety valve." The government now decided to encourage emigration and allow the poor—and their problems—to leave the country. The years 1901 through 1920 saw large numbers of Italians

Immigrating children arriving at Ellis Island are examined by a city health officer in 1911. Health examinations were dreaded because immigrants found to be carrying diseases were usually sent back to their country of origin.

going to North America—over 2 million people between 1901 and 1910. Another 1 million left between 1911 and 1920.

Many Italians who emigrated did not intend to remain permanently in North America. Their idea was to work and save their money in order to return to Italy and buy land. As a result, many early immigrants, especially those in the more populated cities of the northeastern United States, were thought of as temporary citizens. They were looked down on because people felt the Italians were in the U.S. only to make money, and were not fully contributing to the prosperity of the country. Italians had escaped the prejudice of the northern Italians back home, but they ran into a similar brand of discrimination in the New World. ✸

How They Came

For many Italians, traveling to North America was their first trip outside of their native village. Males often traveled first, usually the father and perhaps the oldest son, in order to find work and send money home so the rest of the family could follow.

When it was time for the family to leave, they sold the few possessions they had, taking only necessities with them: clothing, shoes, hats, a coat, and personal items. These they loaded into a handmade wooden trunk. The trunk was large, perhaps five feet long, three feet high, and three feet deep, and well made in order to protect the family's belongings on the long trip. The people would hire a horse-drawn cart to carry the trunk. One man stated, "We had that trunk many, many years. I think I can remember it being in my family even when I got married, and for 25 to 30 years after we got to America."

An Italian woman and her children arrive at Ellis Island in 1905. The long, uncomfortable journey was just the first step in starting a new life in America. Immigrants had to face a barrage of tests and examinations before they were allowed to enter the United States. They often came with little money and few connections.

Highways and automobiles were not in widespread use, like today, and trains only connected the big cities. Many walked much of the way, sleeping where they could. There were no hotels or motels, so they stayed in family homes along the route.

The least expensive route was from Naples to New York City. As a result, Naples was the most popular port city for leaving Italy. Arriving in the port city meant the first part of the journey was over and you were on your way to the New World. It also meant you had to buy a steamship ticket, if you did not already have one, and perhaps wait to board. Some people had to wait weeks to board their ships. They stayed in facilities provided by the shipping companies and operated by **landsmen**. These facilities where the emigrants stayed were often large rooms, shared by up to 100 people. Like the food they were going to find on the ship, the food in these facilities was often a little meat, a few vegetables, bread, butter, garlic, and **herring**. Herring was supposed to prevent seasickness once they got on the boat.

Once on board, most people traveled in the steerage section, which is located in the lowest part of the ship. It is called steerage because it is near the ship's gears, pulleys, and other devices that make up the equipment that steered the ship. Travelers in this section were kept apart from the other passengers, who were from the wealthier classes.

The places where people stayed during the voyage were called compartments. A typical steerage compartment at the time was six or eight feet high, with two or three sets of metal bunks where the people

Cheap steerage accommodations encouraged hundreds of thousands of people to emigrate from Europe. These passengers had to provide food for their families for up to 2 months, however, and the journey was often rough, making the passengers seasick.

slept. Compartments had no windows and air circulation was poor. Women and men stayed in separate areas, but children remained with their mothers. Toilet facilities were primitive and rarely cleaned. Mingled with the other smells from the hold of the ship, the air in steerage had a terrible odor.

Some companies jammed up to 2,000 passengers—men, women, and children—into the steerage sections of their larger ships.

A ship full of immigrants passes the Statue of Liberty in New York Harbor. The welcoming sight of this symbolic statue was often the first thing immigrating foreigners saw as they came to America.

The Atlantic Ocean is fierce, especially in the winter months when storms almost constantly whip the water with their howling winds. These storms create huge waves that constantly lashed the ship. This made for a long, cold, and often dangerous voyage.

For many passengers, seasickness was a constant problem. Few had traveled on the water for long periods of time, and almost none were used to the constant motion caused by the rolling waves. An Italian immigrant named Frank Santoni recalled, "My mother was sick one night, and she moaned all night, practically. Sometime in the wee hours of the morning she asked me to please go upstairs and get some water for her, as you had to go up perhaps 10 or 12 steps in order to get to the upper part of the boat, to get water, and that's what I did. It was just about dawn, and as I got to the last step, somehow or another the latched doors opened. It seemed to me I was just about to 'meet the water;' the boat was heaving on that side and it felt to me as if I was just about able to reach the water. I was only seasick twice, that was one of the times. I got so sick, after that, I don't remember whether I got the water."

The law required that the shipping companies examine, vaccinate, and disinfect passengers before they were allowed to board the ships. Although the companies complied with the law, they usually did a poor job of this, their main objective being to sell tickets and collect money. Consequently, many people who could have solved their medical problems before coming to North America were sent home because they were found to have unacceptable health conditions. Many who had left their

Fiorello H. La Guardia was an American government official in Fiume, Italy from 1903 to 1906. Seeing the result that careless medical examinations were having on the poor emigrants, he decided to do something about it. He insisted that the medical exams the shipping companies gave to the emigrants before leaving Italy were thorough and complete. Although this upset the companies because it was more expensive for them, La Guardia was determined that the medical procedures be followed. Because of this, the number of people who had to return to Italy was far less than in other countries. The Italian government, which was encouraging emigration during this time, officially adopted La Guardia's policy in 1908. Other countries also began requiring more thorough medical examinations, and in 1924, the United States made it mandatory that the main medical examination be administered before emigrants left their home countries. La Guardia, an Italian American, later served as mayor of New York City.

families and had sailed thousands of miles across the ocean were bitterly disappointed to find out they had to return.

Shipping company officials also asked questions regarding marital status, financial resources, political and religious ties, country of origin, and final destination. A wrong answer might mean you could not travel any farther and had to return home. Not only were emigrants facing an entirely new way of life in a strange land where they often did not know anyone and did not speak the language, they also lived in a state of fear from the time they left their homes until they landed and cleared the medical exams and questioning by officials. ❋

Steelworkers test molten steel in this work by American painter Gerrit Albertus Beneker. On arriving in North America, many Italian immigrants were relegated to doing grueling physical labor for meager pay.

What They Did

Before the New World became accessible to people, Italians often migrated to parts of Europe in search of work and opportunity for a better life. For instance, the Waldensians, a northern Italian religious sect, had been migrating to France seasonally since the Middle Ages. When the United States and Canada opened to settlement, young men crossed the ocean in spring and worked through summer until late in the fall. During this time, they saved and sent extra money home. The young men returned as heroes to their homes in Italy, where they spent the winter months.

There were only a few thousand Italians in North America in the mid 1800s, most of whom had emigrated from northern Italy. Many were craftsmen or middle-class merchants who dreamed of returning to Italy when it became united and free. Southern Italians by the thousands began to arrive in the New World toward the end of the 1800s after conditions in their native country became intolerable.

The northern Italians who came to the New World tended to have more education and appeared more like the majority of the *populace*, with light skin and hair color. This was because they had descended from the *Germanic* peoples of Europe. Southern Italians, on the other hand, came primarily from farm communities where education was not available to them. They tended to have the physical characteristics—darker skin and hair color—of the French, Moorish, Greek, Arab, and Spanish

Frank Sinatra gained popularity as a singer in the 1940s and sustained his success for five decades. Sinatra's mother was an immigrant from northern Italy; his father was from southern Italy.

peoples from whom they were descended. When large numbers of southern Italians began to arrive in the New World, they received little help and encouragement from the northern Italians who had already settled there. This was a result of age-old prejudices and a *superiority complex* some northern Italians had developed.

Upon arrival, southern Italians often had to settle for the nonskilled jobs considered undesirable by others. They were employed in work gangs, fixing streets, and constructing buildings. Italian laborers helped build New York City's skyscrapers and its subway system. Italians took jobs in the coal mines of West Virginia and Kentucky, and worked at mining gold, silver, and copper in the West. They assisted in building the railroads, both in Canada and the United States. Many worked in the stockyards and meat packing plants of Chicago. The steel mills of Michigan and Pennsylvania employed Italians, as did the textile mills

 36

of New England. Many Italian women remained in New York and took jobs in the garment industry.

Because they did not know anyone when they arrived and often could not speak English, many Italians had to work through a contract agent, called a *padrone*, in order to find a job. The process started even before the immigrants arrived. The *padrone* traveled to Italy to search for men and women who wanted to go to the New World. He promised to help by making the travel arrangements and finding them work.

Unfortunately, the shrewd *padrone*, posing as a friend, often took advantage of the hopeful newcomers by charging them from $1 to $10 for his services. Considering the price of a ticket on an ocean liner cost immigrants between $10 and $15, it is easy to see the *padrone* was making a large profit. As soon as they could, the

Frank Santoni was a small boy when he left Italy for the United States with his mother, two brothers, one sister, and a cousin. He says, "I remember that we left in a cart, a two-wheeled cart with a big home-made trunk...And we started off for Palermo, which is about 40 miles away, with one horse and a driver...We stayed overnight in a small town, where we slept in a stable. We started the same way the next morning, and we got to Palermo. I do remember that we took a small launch. We hopped onto it—there was no such thing as a dock. And the Mediterranean [Sea] was very rough. We had to travel some distance to get to the boat. It was an overnight trip. And I remember so well that there was really a lot of crying going on because of the frightfulness of the Mediterranean. Now this boat was not a boat to come across the ocean. You had to go to Naples—there you take the ship."

immigrants found work on their own rather than deal with the *padrone*. Those who had good business sense started their own enterprises. Some opened small shops or restaurants; some became farmers; others went into the construction or food distribution business.

Amadeo Obici was 12 years old when he arrived in the United States. He began to sell fruit from a corner stand when he was 17. His specialty was roasted peanuts. The business grew and prospered, and eventually became the Planter's Peanut Company.

Other industrious Italians started wineries, vineyards, and citrus farms. In 1881, Andrea Sbarbaro founded the Italian Swiss Colony winery. In 1891, Marco Fontana started the California Fruit Packing Company. Later, the company changed its name to Del Monte and became one of the largest fruit and vegetable canning companies in the world.

Second-generation Italian-American Amadeo Peter Giannini wanted to help his fellow Italians, because banks were discriminating against them and refusing to give them loans. In San Francisco in 1904, Giannini opened the Bank of Italy. It eventually became the Bank of America, one of the world's largest financial institutions.

Italians helped the new cities in North America become more refined in music and art. Lorenzo de Ponte established opera in New York City. Giuseppe Ceracchi was a well-known Italian-American

Signs for Italian restaurants dominate this district of North Beach in San Francisco, California. Italians celebrate their rich culture by continuing Old World traditions of preparing and serving authentic Italian cuisine.

Known as the Yankee Clipper, Joe DiMaggio helped the New York Yankees win nine World Series championships. In this photograph he is surrounded by his family; his nieces and nephew sit on his lap, and he is smiling at his mother. A strong, supportive family life is highly valued by Italians and Italian Americans.

sculptor who also helped create the official seals, emblems, and *insignias* for the government of the United States. Arturo Toscanini is famous as the orchestra director for the New York Metropolitan Opera Company, where the great Italian tenor, Enrico Caruso, often sang beginning in 1903. Frank Capra, a Hollywood film director, immigrated to the United States with his family when he was six years old. His movies, many of which became classics, include *It Happened One Night*, which won four Academy Awards, *Mr. Smith Goes to*

Washington, and *It's a Wonderful Life*. An Italian nun, Mother Frances Xavier Cabrini, became the first citizen of North America to be named a saint in the Roman Catholic church.

Notable second-generation Italian Americans include Frank Sinatra, the famous singer who also became a well-known actor; actress Anne Bancroft, born Anne Marie Italiano in New York City; and Joe DiMaggio, a famous baseball player who helped the New York Yankees win nine World Series championships. ✹

Of the millions of Italians who arrived in the United States during the late 19th century, many stayed in New York and other large cities of the east coast. Italian laborers played a large part in the construction of New York City's skyline. Many also worked to build the city's network of subways.

5 Where They Settled

Most of the Italians who arrived in North America after 1865 settled in the northeastern part of the United States and southeastern Canada. A majority of these people settled in the cities. In Italian neighborhoods, often called "Little Italies," one could find Italian food, almost everyone spoke Italian, and there was a *predominance* of Italian culture. Italian language newspapers were published, and people with Italian roots owned and operated many of the banks, stores, and restaurants.

It was natural for newcomers to America to feel comfortable living in an area where so much was familiar. The Little Italy area of New York City was first choice for many immigrants, with its concentration of Italians around Mulberry Street and the Lower East Side. Boston, Buffalo, Cleveland, Philadelphia, Pittsburgh, and Toronto also had Little Italy neighborhoods that grew up in the more affordable areas.

The scene on Mulberry Street in New York City around 1900. Mulberry Street and the surrounding area was the section of New York most Italian immigrants were drawn to, mainly because other Italian Americans had settled here.

In 1850, there were 100 Italians in the city of Chicago. Most of them came from the Italian Riviera area of northern Italy. By 1898, there were 25,000 Italians, most of whom were immigrants from southern Italy.

Northern Italians founded the Italian settlement in Chicago. In the 1880s, large numbers of southern Italians began to arrive in the city, drawn by an abundance of jobs in the area's meat processing plants, farm equipment factories, and the railroads. Most of these new residents settled in the city's Little Italy, which was located near the downtown business district of present-day Chicago.

Successful newspaperman Generoso Pope wanted to help his fellow Italian Americans. He joined with a wealthy friend to offer low-interest loans so poor immigrants could buy land and start farms in Vineland, New Jersey. In the 1880s, Vineland was the largest Italian community outside of Italy. Today, Italians continue to farm in Vineland, where they make up a large percentage of the population.

In Arkansas, Italians founded an agricultural community called Tontitown (after explorer Enrico de Tonti). It began in 1898 with 900 acres, and today remains a successful farming community.

In California, Italians settled in the Los Angeles,

A man works at a cheese shop in New York City's Little Italy. Ethnically-concentrated neighborhoods were important to immigrants, who didn't want to lose their heritage as they adapted to life in the United States.

Napa, Fresno, San Mateo, Stockton, and San Francisco areas where they planted many beautiful orchards, vineyards, and gardens. San Francisco also has a Little Italy near Fisherman's Wharf, where Italians benefited from a successful fishing industry. ✺

45

6 Influences and Attitudes

The Roman Catholic Church and the Mafia have been strong influences on the image of Italians in North America. This influence began even before the immigrants arrived.

Until 1873, the Catholic Church was the largest single landowner in Italy. Most of the peasants viewed the priests and other church officials as part of the nobility, which for the most part did not care about helping the poor, but only about taking advantage of them.

A choir standing with a statue of the Virgin Mary performs at an Italian street festival in New York City. Many Italian Americans are Roman Catholic, and their strong religious views are evident in their celebrations and religious observances.

One result of this was that the people put more faith in the church's saints than in its bishops and priests.

Southern Italy is a mixture of different cultures. The Catholicism that developed there reflected this *diversity* and was a combination of various symbols, values, and traditional ideas. This unique outlook helped Italian peasants cope with the problems and challenges of their lives. Rather than consult church officials, they often prayed to the saints who were such an important element in the church and their lives. They also honored them by observing "feast days," each dedicated to a particular saint. The people celebrated the feast days by thinking about that saint's *virtues*, praying, telling stories, and eating and drinking in the saint's memory. The peasants also celebrated "holy days," which were days that marked special events in church history and occurrences in the lives of saints. People paraded through the streets carrying statues with money pinned to the images. There was also food and music. The conditions of poverty and hopelessness in Italy at the time helped make the church one of the few stable parts of the peasants' lives.

When Italians began to arrive in great numbers in North America, the Irish dominated the Catholic Church. The officials of the church and the congregations were mostly Irish. They thought of the Italian Catholics as too *flamboyant* and *mystical*, and openly made fun of them. Naturally, friction developed. Soon many Irish Catholic priests would not allow Italians to attend their churches, putting pressure on them to abandon their ways of worship. The clergy also attempted to influence Italian children who were attending Catholic school. They tried to force them to give up their Italian customs and traditions. This caused many families to stop sending their children to Catholic schools. They began to ask for their own, separate churches, schools, and *parishes*. The bishops were not in favor of this at first, but eventually granted their requests. Catholic officials established separate parishes, such as New York City's Saint Anthony of Padua parish, where Italians could practice their faith according to their own customs. Many first-generation Italians joined with their neighbors to donate the money and labor needed to build and organize their churches.

So in the Italian communities of the New World, as in the Old World, the church became one of the main *focal* points of family and community life. Traditional customs and rituals blended with church and family activities, such as weddings, baptisms, funerals, and feast days. In the early 1900s, Protestant groups succeeded in converting some Italian Catholics to their faith, but the majority of Italians remained Catholic. Second- and third-generation Italians may not follow Catholic traditions as strictly as their parents and grandparents, but an Italian Catholic living today in North America who marries outside his or her *ethnic* group is still most likely to wed another Catholic.

A more negative organization traditionally associated with Italian Americans is the Mafia. The Mafia image is a complex blend of fact, myth, fear, and imagination historians say goes back long before Italians came to the New World.

People living on the island of Sicily used the word *mafia* to

People who study crime statistics report that Italians who belong to the Mafia make up less than .0001 percent of the Italian population in North America. However, Americans are fascinated by the Mafia, as shown by the success of books like *The Godfather* and *Wiseguy*, movies like *Goodfellas* and *Casino*, and television shows like *The Sopranos*.

mean a general distrust of people outside of one's own family, regarding them as unimportant. They also used the word to describe small groups of bandits that roamed the countryside. The code by which these groups lived was outside the law at the time, but the group members felt it was justified because the government and the courts were **corrupt**. This type of behavior, based on an eleventh-century **Norman** code of **chivalry**, said that justice could be given by friends and family, backed up by a "code of silence," which meant members would not reveal the names of other group members to officials. Centuries ago, the men on Sicily often banded together to protect their loved ones and their possessions from invaders. Others paid these groups to protect them also, which fostered the idea of "protection money." Romantic storytellers wove these facts into colorful adventures of a group that operated in secret and had far-reaching powers and authority. The stories were highly believable to the poor and uneducated, which made up most of the population.

In the 1880s, in the town of Andalusia in Spain, the police announced the discovery of a secret society known as the Black Hand. Supposedly, the people who belonged to this organization had sworn to murder the landowners of the area. It was not long before people began to associate Italians, some of whom were involved with **anarchist** activities at the time, with the Spanish people who were supposed to be members of the Black Hand. Similar sounding names and physical appearances between the Spanish and the Italians made

In 1920, Nicola Sacco and Bartolomeo Vanzetti, both of whom supported socialism, were arrested for murdering two people and stealing $15,000. Although 16 people testified the men had been nowhere near the scene of the crime, prejudice toward Italians helped convict the two men. After numerous appeals, Sacco and Vanzetti were put to death in 1927. The foreman of the jury that convicted the two men referred to them as "dagoes." In the final statement addressed to the court, Vanzetti wrote, "I am suffering because I was a radical and indeed I am a radical. I have suffered because I am an Italian and indeed I am an Italian." The two men were exonerated more than 50 years later by Massachusetts governor Michael Dukakis.

Italian-born anarchists Bartolomeo Vanzetti (center) and Nicola Sacco (right) sit handcuffed to a guard in Dedham, Massachusetts.

During the *Prohibition* era in the United States, which lasted from 1920 through 1933, Al Capone made headlines as the reputed head of organized crime in Chicago. Capone was finally sent to jail for not paying taxes.

this association easier. The reality of this group was never proven, but the story helped make great headlines in the newspapers.

There are problems with this historical view of the Mafia compared to the modern version. First, the Sicilian Mafia did not have a central organization, but consisted of scattered groups of people operating on their own. Second, it was almost entirely a rural *phenomenon*—these groups banded together for protection against invaders in the remote areas of Sicily. The image of the modern Mafia is portrayed as a centrally organized urban group.

All of this has combined to form our current idea of the Mafia. It is natural, as some *sociologists* have suggested, to think of the criminal element as having an organization, much like labor has unions, business has professional affiliations, and the government and the military have their structures. They also strongly suggest that the producers of movies, television, books, and magazines have benefited greatly from promoting this "Godfather" image. So while it is obvious that certain types of individuals often commit crime, those individuals are not limited to a certain class of people or nationality.

The Italians came to North America a disadvantaged group

because they had less education and tended to be poorer. Added to this was public opinion that had often been turned against them because they were easy targets for authors and newspaper writers, who portrayed anyone with an Italian background as tied to organized crime. This image is changing, as society becomes more educated and more discriminating in the news and entertainment to which they subscribe.

Today, most Italian Americans are descendants of people who emigrated from southern Italy. Many of these people came in the last

Al Capone glares at the camera in this intimidating mug shot. Capone was the most powerful and notorious gangster of the 1920s. He was finally imprisoned, not for murder or extortion, but for federal income tax evasion in 1931.

years of the 19th century and the early part of the 20th century.

World War I (1914–1918), the passage of restrictive immigration laws during the 1920s, and the Second World War (1939–1945) slowed Italian immigration to the United States. However, after immigration restrictions were lifted in 1965, the number of Italians moving to America increased again. During the 1970s, 1980s, and 1990s, more than 100,000 people emigrated from Italy to the United States. According to the 2000 U.S. Census, there are more than 20 million Americans of Italian descent. The Italian-Canadian population is estimated at nearly 1.8 million.

North America has proven to be a land of opportunity for many of the immigrants who came to its shores. This is especially true for many of the Italian peasants who had nothing when they left Italy and arrived in the United States and Canada with only their hopes and dreams. The success of Italian Americans has come through hard work and persistence. As Thomas Sowell wrote in his book *Ethnic America*, "Some early Italian Americans may have summarized it best when they held up the hands with which they earned their living and said, 'America is *here–this* is America.'" ✹

Famous Italian Americans

Anne Bancroft actress

Mother Frances Xavier Cabrini Roman Catholic saint

Enrico Caruso opera singer

Giuseppe Ceracchi artist

Francis Ford Coppola film director

Joe DiMaggio baseball star

Geraldine Ferraro politician

Enrico Fermi nuclear physicist

Marco Fontana founder of the Del Monte company

Amadeo Peter Giannini founder of the Bank of America

Rudolph W. Guiliani former mayor of New York City

Vince Lombardi legendary football coach

Rocky Marciano undefeated heavyweight boxing champion

Amadeo Obici founder of the Planter's Peanut Company

Mario Puzo novelist

Caesar Rodney American colonial leader

Andrea Sbarbaro founder of the Italian Swiss Colony winery

Antonin Scalia justice of the U.S. Supreme Court

Frank Sinatra popular singer and actor

Arturo Toscanini classical music conductor

Rudolph Valentino romantic movie star

Chronology

1848 The number of Italians in North America is around 10,000.

1871 Italian soldiers march into Rome; Italy is declared a free and unified country.

1873 The Roman Catholic Church is the largest landowner in Italy.

1881 The first large groups from Italy begin emigrating to the New World. Over the next 40 years, almost four million Italians come to North America.

1891 Marco Fontana starts the California Fruit Packing Company, later Del Monte, one of the largest fruit and vegetable canning companies in the world.

1898 Italians establish the agricultural community of Tontitown in Arkansas.

1903 Enrico Caruso makes his debut at the Metropolitan Opera House in New York City.

1917 The United States Congress passes a law requiring that immigrants know how to read and write English, severely limiting the number of poor people allowed into the country.

1921 Nicola Sacco and Bartolomeo Vanzetti are arrested in Boston.

1924 Legislation is passed that further restricts the number of immigrants allowed into the United States.

1931 Al Capone is convicted of income tax evasion and sentenced to 11 years in prison.

1938 Enrico Fermi is awarded the Nobel Prize for his work in nuclear physics.

1946 The Catholic Church declares Mother Cabrini a saint, the first person in North America so honored.

1967 Italians living in Toronto make up the city's largest non-British Old World group.

1984 Second-generation Italian-American Geraldine Ferraro becomes the first woman to be nominated for the office of vice president of the United States.

2003 The Italian-American population of the United States is estimated at more than 20 million.

Glossary

Absentee landlord a land owner who lives away from his property and rents his land to tenant farmers.

Anarchist one who uses violent means to overthrow the established order.

Aristocracy an upper class in a society usually made up of the nobility.

Bureaucrat a government official who follows a routine in a mechanical, unimaginative manner.

Chivalry behaving like a gallant or distinguished gentleman.

Commodity a basic necessity, often food.

Corrupt low in value or quality, taking bribes, evil.

Cutlery tools used to prepare and serve food, such as knives.

Diversity composed of distinct unlike elements.

Emigrate to move away from one's home country to settle in another country.

Ethnic a group of people that has common customs, language, history, and so on.

Flamboyant too showy.

Focal of, relating to, being, or having a focus.

Germanic people descended from areas in Europe that include Iceland, Norway, Sweden, Denmark, Germany, and Holland.

Herring a fish that is usually preserved for consumption by salting or smoking.

Insignia an official drawing or design.

Landsmen men who perform work on land for shipping companies.

Mystical beyond human comprehension, mysterious, magical.

Norman characteristic of the Scandinavian people who occupied Normandy (part of present-day France) in the 10th century.

Parish a church district.

Phenomenon a rare or significant fact or circumstance.

Populace the masses, or common people.

Profitable yielding advantageous return or results.

Prohibition the period in the United States (1920-1933) when the manufacture, transportation, and sale of alcoholic beverages was illegal.

Predominance most noticeable.

Repression silencing ideas, speech, or other types of expression.

Republican a type of government whose people elect others to represent them in government activities, trusting them with their power.

Resigned to have given up.

Sociologist a person who studies the beliefs, values, customs, and so on of the various groups that make up humanity.

Steerage a section of inferior accommodations in a passenger ship for passengers paying the lowest fare.

Stratified layered or multilayered; groups of people organized as to education, birth, or income.

Superiority complex exaggerated self-importance that manifests as arrogance; an attitude that is actually compensating for feelings of being inferior.

Tariffs taxes and other obligations, especially those a government places on imported items.

Virtue excellent character qualities, such as courage, goodness, or strength.

Further Reading

Coan, Peter M. *Ellis Island Interviews: In Their Own Words.* New York: Facts on File, 1997.

Di Franco, J. Philip. *The Italian Americans.* New York: Chelsea House Publishers, 1988.

Jacobs, Nancy R., Rein, Mei Ling, and Seigel, Mark S. eds., *Immigration and Illegal Aliens–Burden or Blessing?* Wylie: Information Plus, 1999.

Lombardo, Anthony. *The Italians in America.* Chicago: Claretian Publications, 1973.

Moquin, Wayne, with Charles Van Doren and Francis A.J. Ianni, eds. *A Documentary History of the Italian Americans.* New York: Praeger Publishers, 1974.

Nugent, Walter. *Crossings: The Great Trans-Atlantic Migrations, 1870–1914.* Bloomington: Indiana University Press, 1992.

Tracing Your Italian-American Ancestors

Carmack, Sharon DeBartolo. *A Genealogist's Guide to Discovering Your Immigrant and Ethnic Ancestors.* Cincinnati: Betterway Books, 2000.

Colletta, John Philip. *Finding Italian Roots: The Complete Guide for Americans.* Baltimore: Genealogical Publishing Co., 1996.

Nelson, Lynn. *A Genealogist's Guide to Discovering Your Italian Ancestors.* Cincinnati: Betterway Books, 1997.

Internet Resources

http://www.census.gov

The official website of the U.S. Bureau of the Census contains information about the most recent census taken in 2000.

http://www.statcan.ca/start.html

The website for Canada's Bureau of Statistics, which includes population information updated for the most recent census in July 2001.

http://www.ins.gov

The Immigration and Naturalization Service Web site provides information on becoming a citizen, one's rights and responsibilities, as well as forms, fees, and other information.

http://www.cis.org

The Center for Immigration Studies Web site is aimed at expanding public knowledge and understanding of the need for a broad immigration policy.

http://www.ellisislandrecords.org

This Web site is devoted to the history of Ellis Island and the immigrants who came through its doors.

Index

Photo Credits

Contributors

Barry Moreno has been librarian and historian at the Ellis Island Immigration Museum and the Statue of Liberty National Monument since 1988. He is the author of *The Statue of Liberty Encyclopedia*, which was published by Simon & Schuster in October 2000. He is a native of Los Angeles, California. After graduation from California State University at Los Angeles, where he earned a degree in history, he joined the National Park Service as a seasonal park ranger at the Statue of Liberty; he eventually became the monument's librarian. In his spare time, Barry enjoys reading, writing, and studying foreign languages and grammar. His biography has been included in *Who's Who Among Hispanic Americans*, *The Directory of National Park Service Historians*, *Who's Who in America*, and *The Directory of American Scholars*.

Richard A. Bowen is a Wisconsin author, whose books include *The Art of Hearing: Seven Practical Methods for Improving Your Hearing*, *Meeting Your Match–His Story*, and *Spirit and Nature*, a book of verse. He is co-owner of Ariadne Publishers and editor of "Spiritual Awakenings" quarterly.